Life in the Low Place

a Poetic Journey

As Told by Mena

Prepared by Ebony Nicole Smith Consulting, LLC | website: https://ebonynicolesmith.com

Editor: CaTyra Polland | For the Love of Words | pollandllc.com

Photographer: Kameron Ashford | Blank Kanvas Photography and Cinematography

Cover Designer: Dynasty Cover Designs

Scripture references: Holy Bible, New Living Translation copyright 1996, 2004, 2007, 2015 by Tyndale House Foundation.

Printed in the United States of America

First Edition 2021

ISBN: 978-0-578-93076-3

Contents

Dedication

For you, "*The sun shall not smite thee by day,*
nor the moon by night."

Psalm 121:6

Acknowledgments

I would like to thank God for breathing purpose into my life. My very existence is the manifestation of a promise and a reminder that he makes all things beautiful. I must also thank my parents, Eric and Myreen Tross for being the vehicles God used to bring me into this world. Mom & Dad, I know traffic was heavy but I'm here now! I have not yet "arrived," but I am allowing the world to journey with me as I grow. Many of these pieces were written from childhood through my late teen years up until now. So, thank you for encouraging my freedom to create and express myself in ways you didn't always understand. You guys just knew that I was just a tad bit different.

To my coach Ebony Nicole Smith, may the God of hope fill you with all joy and peace as you trust in Him, so that you may overflow with hope by the

power of the Holy Spirit. You have pushed me, encouraged me, and guided me through this project with joy even while life was happening on your own end. I am excited for your next season!

I would be remiss if I did not add this Super Woman into my acknowledgements. Dr. Ashley Cross, I am extremely grateful to have you as one of my leaders. The goal setting meeting we had in January changed my life. Just when I wanted to go into panic mode, you helped me to see that a little hope can go a long way. I could not have published this book without you!

To the one whom my soul loves, my husband Donnivon Dodd, I can't thank you enough! You have challenged me in ways that I didn't know were possible. With you, I've learned the value of persisting and producing from a healed perspective. From late nights to early mornings, you sat up just to hear my heart. Your love has fueled every one of my dreams. You are my #1 supporter and my biggest fan! I love you.

And lastly, to the future, you will be more than what we can imagine and greater than any of our expectations. I speak to you!

"Did you hear about the rose that grew from a crack in the concrete?" Tupac Shakur

I remember the first time I read this poem in its entirety. I was compelled by the way Shakur raised awareness of something that defies the science of reasoning or thought. How likely is it that a frail, insubstantial, and minuscule plant interrupts a solid cement surface? You see it's not necessarily the plant that has the power to grow through the concrete, it's the roots that do the pushing. As the root system stretches and matures it seeks to use the opposition as expansion. To the average person, this circumstance could be bothersome but through the eyes of hope, it is simply life-giving.

Life in the Low Place is a compilation of poems I've written from the age of eight until now while journeying through very dark and tough spaces. I started creative writing and journaling in 2003. I immediately realized that it was my safe place. **Writing is how I worship.** So, although I was swimming and drowning simultaneously in the sanctuary of my center, The Lord anointed me to scribe. What I felt was not always for me and did not always have a sound but, I always had a voice when I put it on paper.

Through the distinct meaningful elements of writing, I discovered that my words conveyed the hearts of so many of those in quest of comfort, peace, redemption and so much more.

iv

The Rose & the Concrete

"Did you hear about the rose that grew from
a crack in the concrete?"
Tupac Shakur

I remember the first time I read this poem in its entirety. I was compelled by the way Shakur raised awareness of something that defies our very own science of reasoning or thought. How likely is it for a frail, insubstantial, and minuscule plant to interrupt a solid cement surface?

You see it's not necessarily the plant that has the power to grow through the concrete; it's the roots that do the pushing. As the root system stretches and matures it seeks to use the opposition as expansion. To the average person, this event of circumstance could be bothersome but through the eyes of hope, it is simply life-giving.

Life in the Low Place is a compilation of poems I've written from the age of eight up until now while journeying through very dark and tough spaces. In 2003, I started creative writing and began to journal the process. I immediately found that it was my safe place.

Life in the Low Place: a Poetic Journey

Writing for me has served as worship. So although I was swimming and drowning simultaneously in the sanctuary of my center, The Lord had anointed me to scribe. What I felt was not always for me and did not always have a sound but, I always had a voice when I put it on paper.

Through the distinct meaningful elements of writing, I discovered that my words conveyed the hearts of so many of those in quest of comfort, peace, redemption and so much more.

This is me being a rose and pushing through the crack in the concrete. Come and take a poetic journey with me.

Saturday

2 Timothy 2:22

A Friday night smile met the break of dawn with eagerness.

She resumed doing what she knew was wrong.

It felt both pleasing and wrong, but she was told no right. Repeating to all goodnight, just to meet Saturday mornings again.

There was no way to comprehend or undo what Saturdays had marked.

There is a stillness yet still no peace.

There is a heartbeat where there should not be.

A sense of shame beyond what people see.

She hasn't even reached double digits in age.

She is writing beyond the pages from what she doesn't know to be true yet but half of her lives while the other half is barely breathing.

There is a suffocation of secrets that those cartoon character blankets hold and fruit of betrayal, confusion, and sadness that refuse to be washed away.

I don't know when Saturday began but I know that one day Saturday will end, and I hope it's soon.

Life in the Low Place: a Poetic Journey

_____

_____

_____

_____

_____

_____

_____

_____

_____

_____

_____

_____

_____

_____

Aschenputtel.

Esther 4:14

People notice you because you are different.
And in your humility, far from the crowd like
a sore thumb, you stick out. You STAND out.
What is it you've been wishing for? Favor
from rulers who seek to sift you as wheat?
Don't you ever--
Do not desire what they have or what they
give.
Charm is deceptive, and beauty fades.
But a woman who fears the Lord is to be
praised.
What you have comes from the inward.
It is from the abundance of the heart that
your mouth speaks. And even so from your heart
flows the springs of life.
Utilize what you see, use what you have.
You are not little ashes; you are like
Cinderella.
Awaiting your appointed time to put on that
lost glass slipper. Not a damsel, not a victim but a
victor.
Not a maid, not a slave but a daughter.
You are like Esther, in transition from pit to
palace. Appointed for such a time as this.
You are not little ashes.

Life in the Low Place: a Poetic Journey

_____

_____

_____

_____

_____

_____

_____

_____

_____

_____

_____

_____

Do Not Let Your Heart be Troubled

Exodus 33:14

As for me, there were times when my
admission was, "Lord, I have grown faint."
   Though I chose to live through it, so a smile
each day I painted
   -- upon my face with eyes like slits protruding
invisible despair.
   These eyes let out water when things had
gone a blunder, tears falling everywhere.

   Though tired, these tears today are not tears
of disappointment, these are not even tears of
despondency.
   These are the tears of tenacity.
   The tears that are watering the garden of my
labor.
   The same tears the Lord collected in His
bottle.
   He has numbered my wanderings and kept a
record of my misery.
   For I have left the wilderness
   There, then, and here now from that to this.
   So, is ignorance really bliss?
   Or is this bliss found looking to the cross
   seeing the profundity of God's mercy fulfilled
through His Son.
   I do not have to be troubled by this life.
Christ endured so that I could live.

_____

_____

_____

_____

_____

_____

_____

_____

_____

_____

_____

_____

_____

Bring to Bay

Psalm 86:6

If my bones were being gambled for luck in a dark alley on a dark night,

Would it be the same inclination and desire that's sinners reborn believe will bless the just and the upright?

I cry out for the God of hope to save me!

My posture is imperfect, and my weight is alright. I'm pretty small to be carrying this weight though. So, will the wait be alright?

I CRY OUT for the God of hope to comfort me!

I anticipated the perfect time to lay my burdens down, but did I bow too soon?

I became acquainted with the pain hanging on to attention that brokenness brought me but now empty is the room.

Friends are few.

How funny, it's quite hysterical that in my surrender the crowd is thin.

I yield to depression, I submit to the Lord my anxiety, I relent the influence of suicide. Yet the lights are still dim.

I cry out to the God of love, "Please, raise my head!"

Life in the Low Place: a Poetic Journey

_____

_____

_____

_____

_____

_____

_____

_____

_____

_____

_____

_____

_____

Bad Thinking

Philippians 4:8

Some days I feel like nothing.
Not too low but never even almost too high.
Not even in the middle though either.
Not good enough.
Not smart enough
Certainly not pretty enough but that's the
least of my concerns.
Not healthy, and my legs get too hairy.
Not fast enough.
Not educated enough.
Too raw. Too unfiltered.
Too candid. Too optimistic.
Too soft. Too quiet.
I don't fit in --
too short and too thin.
Can I exist with the air?
.. I mean there is life there, in the oxygen--
because there's pressure in the way that I
think..
about myself
because what's on a shelf
is what God says about me
I must haven't fully agreed
 because I go back and forth between what He
said and what I see so coherently.
This is bad, really bad
this way of thinking that is.
Because the Lord is--
good and His love endures
And God's not a man that He should lie even
the son of man that He should repent.

Life in the Low Place: a Poetic Journey

So, what is it?
why can't I commit -- His words to my heart?
because He was there from the start
from when I took my first breath
 and when He rose from His death
But this is hard for me.

Life in the Low Place: a Poetic Journey

_____

_____

_____

_____

_____

_____

_____

_____

_____

_____

_____

_____

_____

I Know You Hear Me

Psalm 61:1-2

Lord, tonight I have to write to you. My lips
cannot utter what I feel.

And although my feelings are valid, they may
not always be true and real.

Father, I am losing it.

And although I hate sob stories

I'm weeping excessively well knowing that I
can give my all to you.

The good, the bad, the ugly, and indifferent

Father, You're the one who mends hearts,
the one who regulates minds,

So, Father, please shepherd these emotions.

I'm begging you. Please teach me how to live
again.

I've been going through the motions.

Life has happened while I've been busy
making plans and I am too weak to contend.

I am writing you emptying out what is left
here. Can you hear me?!

I'm not sure what I've lost on the way to
freedom but I'm certain that I can find it in you.
So, can I pull up on you tonight?

I want to be on the altar laying prostrate at
your feet.

Can I park here? I sped past the boulevard of
brokenness just to make it here on time before I
lose anything else.

Life in the Low Place: a Poetic Journey

This is no joke, I have spent the majority of
my lifetime feeling alone, so can I build my home,
in you?!
I know that you are the giver of peace so
breathe your order here, in the life of my mind, in
this life of mine.
I know you hear me.

_____

_____

_____

_____

_____

_____

_____

_____

_____

_____

_____

_____

_____

Return to Sender

1 John 1:9

You are the leading force that stirs my hands to raise.
Whether in surrender or in victory
You are the wind beneath my wings
I am learning how to raise a hallelujah, even when what I'm experiencing seems bigger than little ol' me. You are the strength when my knees buckle and my "Yes" gets weak.
It is You who keeps me from stumbling, and Lord I don't want to stumble anymore over the same things,
because they tend to bring, they tend to breed,
they tend to lead; they tend to invite sin and make it comfortable.

I have double-backed more than once and I am ashamed to say, like a dog returning to his own vomit.
I have gotten dressed in those same filthy rags You cleansed me from

And if I'm honest I was so close to turning into a pillar of salt.
I spun the block more than once in the same area You delivered me from, and I need Your help.
You are the shaking force that softens my heart to feel.

Whether crying in anguish or in relief Your caution and my conviction is what I pray never leaves me.

Life in the Low Place: a Poetic Journey

Lord, I Need You.

1 Peter: 1:13

I'm writing this small because my insecurities
seem really big tonight.
I'm getting really quiet because my
insecurities seem really loud and really right.
So, I'm writing to express. But I'm writing to
confess. Why can't I get it right?
What's the issue?
What's really wrong with me?
I feel the pressure and it's taunting me.
Everything I do somehow ends up wrong
I'll be doing really good, but it doesn't last for
too long.
So, I beat myself up with thoughts or words
because from what I just heard my
translation was that I'm "this" I'm "that"
It's "Why this"? "Why that"?
-- I'm the one to blame.
but I'll never play the victim; Because when
it's me, I know it and the impact is like a hit and
run
It's headfirst or heart-first. Yes, heart first
then head.
Then I'll pray and pour it out before I
rehearse it and go to bed.
Rid me of me. Free me from me.
Help me to see me
the way that you see me.
My vision right now is not 2020. It's 120.
So, I need You.

Life in the Low Place: a Poetic Journey

_____

_____

_____

_____

_____

_____

_____

_____

_____

_____

_____

_____

_____

It's 5:40

1 Samuel 16:7

It's 5:40 and I'm thinking about the heart, not
the cheesy heart shape symbol
but the heart that beats, the heart that
breathes, the heart that feels
the organ.
The heart that lives. The real symbol of art.
If only I could take the beauty that's inside of
me, this heart of mine
this love that I have to give
If only I could apply it to my exterior, I'd be
the prettiest woman in the world.
I want that to surface.

_____

_____

_____

_____

_____

_____

_____

_____

_____

_____

_____

_____

The Important Thing About the Color Brown

Revelations 1:15

Black Baby Black Girl Black Woman

    Black is
And black may be
But you don't see color
So of course, you can't see equality

Black Baby Black Boy Black Man
    Black is
And black may be
Innocent or guilty
But what does it matter to you
When you "FEAR FOR YOUR LIFE"
But she was asleep
Her name was Breonna Taylor
    I wonder how this would play out if she were
    white
"I'm unarmed."
"I'm innocent."
I'm not even that dark I'm like cinnamon
But that makes no never mind because I don't
look like you

Sir, please don't kill me
Is it the broken taillight?

Life in the Low Place: a Poetic Journey

The counterfeit bills?
Whatever it is I'll comply
But what I won't do is die
I will not be another hashtag.
I will put brown in my rainbows
I will create brown light. There is such a thing as
brown light
Because Brown highlights how I perceive and
describe the world. I am a color that exists due to
context.
I am not a threat. I am beautiful. I am both a
skittle and an M&M

BLACK BABY BLACK GIRL MAGIC BLACK BOY JOY.

_____

_____

_____

_____

_____

_____

_____

_____

_____

_____

_____

_____

That I May Know Him

Revelation 12:16

Walking through the wilderness, confronting wounds
some self-inflicted, some involuntary
all sharing the same trend-- Abuse.
Walking through the wilderness
though amused by the audacity of enemy
Still confused by the response of those kin to me.
(Because according to them I must've done something terribly wrong to be in this predicament but ok)
I am walking through the wilderness so that I may know Him. I am at the peak of the mountain and the sound is a crescendo of silence as I seek to receive the Lord's peace.
I am in the depth of the valley and the sound is an apex of tranquility as I seek to receive the Lord's comfort.
I am—here not by choice might I add but here I am
I am walking through the wilderness so that I may know Him.
Where is the *Promised Land*?
I'm standing on this promise AND still
yet in the back of my mind what He said I don't really see right now.
I am walking through the wilderness
That I might prove him o 'er and o 'er
And oh, for grace to trust him more
That I may know him.

_____

_____

_____

_____

_____

_____

_____

_____

_____

_____

_____

_____

Confession

1 Peter 5:7

Today my heart feels.

Don't know if it's a good or a bad thing. I'm just thankful that your love heals.

So, I emerge my heart of flesh in Your love that mends.

In Your love that soothes and Your love that defends.

Can we make an exchange today? Your beauty for my ashes because I will gladly take Your joy for my weakness. It's me again, God.

I know that You hear me.

and I know that what You said, I don't really see... right now.

God is not hard of hearing, and He is not reluctant to bless His children

God is not hard of hearing, and He is not reluctant to bless his children

I gotta write this in my head, I'm commanding myself to write it on the tablet of my heart.

Hey God!

Everything I'm feeling can make a really dope art piece. But I'm more interested in the peace that You give.

Life in the Low Place: a Poetic Journey

_____

_____

_____

_____

_____

_____

_____

_____

_____

_____

_____

_____

_____

The Secret Place

Psalm 31:20

Come to the place where worries don't hide.
They're left at the door
Along with your pride.
Hang up your fears, take off your mask.
Remove your cap of shame,
I want you for your past.
You see, I know your biggest secrets and I
know about the lies.
But know that I've come to redeem you.
You are still the prize.
Haven't you felt it? The call on your life.
Haven't you wondered why you don't sleep
at night?
I want all of your attention.
I want your whole heart.
The world tried to consume you.
But you were Mine from the start.
Go ahead and sit, lay, stand, or kneel if you
need to. I promise there isn't anything I
haven't already gotten you through.
Make yourself at home here. Stay for a while.

Yes, I am the Judge but first I am your Father
So no, today there is no trial.
I can hear your cry through those tears
though they don't have a sound
I can see you past the blurred lines my child.
Doesn't it feel good to be found?

_____

_____

_____

_____

_____

_____

_____

_____

_____

_____

_____

_____

_____

_____

Time

Philippians 1:6

Take your time. Be on time—but for the right things. Make time —but for the right things. Time, no man wastes and time—for no man does it wait.

But God is the Master of time. Time is in His hands.

Time starts and stops through Him; He is the Father of time.

So be on time.

But don't rush; take your time.

You don't have much time

but you have all the time you need.

Life in the Low Place: a Poetic Journey

_____

_____

_____

_____

_____

_____

_____

_____

_____

_____

_____

_____

_____

Questions For the Road

Psalm 121:1-2

Lately, I've been hiding. Hiding behind silence. Hiding behind thoughts. Hiding behind the violence.

I never knew I needed space. I didn't know I needed time.

I didn't want to seem needy, so I put "me" off to the side.

The reality is, I will be held accountable for the life that I live.

So, at what point am I secure in who I am called to be? And at what point will I align with what's inside of me?

These are just questions for the road.

There is a vow to be made

walking into this threshold of freedom.

I will not lock myself in.

I will not lock myself out.

As trendy as manifesting is right now.

I know that I only have access to rooms and doors because He is the source, and He is the plug.

He is the property manager and the owner of this building. I cannot do this life on my own.

I will not hold myself up.

And as cool as it sounds to act all tough, I will not hold myself down.

I am not in this alone.

The Lord has my back and fights my battles.

These are just questions for the road. I'm on my way to freedom.

Life in the Low Place: a Poetic Journey

_____

_____

_____

_____

_____

_____

_____

_____

_____

_____

_____

_____

_____

_____

_____

Dear Summer

Numbers 6:24-26

You were rough, but with you, I fell a little deeper in love.

And I hope the time goes by fast with the distance between us

and I swear, I won't take for granted the warm hugs and little bugs that try to kick it when the lights come on and the skies become dark –

but it's still wack.

COVID and killer cops, homicides, amber alerts

and our President hates the color black.

Autumn is approaching,

that means fall is coming but I'm not too mad about that cause when the leaves fall, I'm becoming,

getting rid of the excess, stingy with my accessibility,

sorta like spring cleaning but with pumpkin spice, warm oak scents, sweet potato pie, and distant cousins.

This is a run-on sentence, but I hope you get my letter.

Goodbye Summer 2020

_____

_____

_____

_____

_____

_____

_____

_____

_____

_____

_____

_____

_____

_____

_____

Love Me to Life

1 John 4:9-11

Every day You spare me from Your wrath
after I've bathed in pools of sin
Again, again & again
You consider me Your daughter, Your love, Your
friend
even when I preferred to spend my time trying to
blend in
when You clearly meant for me to stand out.
Still, You loved me.
Still, You love me.
When sin ordered equity with the wages of death,
Your love paid the price
Your love paid the debt
You canceled the payout
You loved me to life.
And on the night, I laid at your feet
bruised and guilty, expecting a hot seat
It was Your love that lifted me--
You lift my head with Your hand.
Yes, you are God the judge but You are God the
Father
You are not like man.
You do not lie.
You love me.

Life in the Low Place: a Poetic Journey

_____

_____

_____

_____

_____

_____

_____

_____

_____

_____

_____

_____

Long Live the Rose

Luke 12:27-28

It's an act of taking one thing and receiving it in return.

The minute that said act takes place, therein you find reciprocity.

And to think there've been moments where a transaction was made or suggested

but turned out to be nothing but a withdrawal but no deposit.

To that, au revoir will be issued!

Tired

of little to no transference.

It was always take, take, take, or give, give, give.

No specific order, however, never quite rewarding or fulfilling.

So, the flower wilted.

The beautiful flower we take from its home to add beauty to our homes.

Yes, that flower wilted.

When a flower wilts from the heat, the flower is now low in energy-

appearance drooping, not as vibrant or radiant as before.

At this point, the flower is said to be damaged.

Its petals are worn from exposure to harsh conditions.

Weather beating.

It's wearing.

Wearing away at its extension from beginning to end.

All of that yet still not corroded.
Blemished but not destroyed.
Flawed but not rotten.
Scarred but not dead.
At times, stiff..
 but it is still a flower.
A seed-bearing plant.
She has the power to reproduce.
Yes, "she" the flower.
Intricately picked out of the number.
selected.
Chosen for your delicate home bouquet but a flower has a purpose.
She bears the brunt of harsh winds
Toughened through the overflow of tears that happen when the clouds' part (we call it rain).
Withstanding through the severe sultriness of the sun; she still stands.

This is a flower.
 Extraordinaire, Strong
Able, Tenacious
Heavy in spunk.
The flower exudes pizzaz.
She has a natural tone of high esteem and delivery.
That wilted, weathered flower, daring and determined.
Carrying the purpose of God's plan, God's love, God's history, and Our future.

This flower is steadfast. Standing firm.
Staying the course
Keeping hard at work to survive.
The rarest yet beautiful flowers survive in the most extreme conditions.
Have you ever seen a plant come back to life?

Life in the Low Place: a Poetic Journey

_____

_____

_____

_____

_____

_____

_____

_____

_____

_____

_____

_____

My Answer is Yes

Matthew 4:18-20

My answer is yes.
When I think about eternity, I often think of a
never-ending yes because a road that's less
traveled often seems endless.
Eons of agreement my yes.
From age to age it's affirmative, yes
Forever though he slays me, unquestionably
yes
That is His promise right?
yes and amen
So, it doesn't matter where I am right now
It doesn't matter where I have been
When He calls, I want to be found standing
without a doubt saying
"Indeed, send me I'll go"
My soul says yes!
It doesn't mean the road will be easy, but He
said He would not leave me.
My mind says yes!
Beyond my own comprehension
Past my own human logic
He takes the foolish things to confound the
wise So, my response is yes.
Though I may not understand, and tears fill
my eyes, in sickness and in health, death won't
even do us part.
I agree to the terms of the conditions, yes.

Life in the Low Place: a Poetic Journey

_____

_____

_____

_____

_____

_____

_____

_____

_____

_____

_____

_____

_____

_____

_____

Speak Well

Psalm 18:21

As a child, I hated being ignored.
It made me feel invisible, and not in a good
way
Have you ever played invisible, and not on a
good day?
So, I started to behave invisibly.
Microscopic almost.
Concealing every part of me to remain unseen.
Maybe I should live small?
No one can see me ,
No one can hear me, but the silence has a
sound.
Insecurity, misconception, self-doubt cranking
as loud as it can behind a wall that's signed, "you
can't see me"!
 But careful you might drown here.
Wallowing in self-pity because no one has
found your voice but neither have you.
Dancing in the heat of scorn while in the seat
of scorn because no one can feel your pain.
But neither can you because you hide it oh so
very well.

I pray that you communicate well today.
God forbid you ignore a person who's already
feeling rejected.
I pray that you converse with the person
you've left on read in your text messages
because you out of all people know how it is to
feel dejected.
You have a voice, so speak well.

Life in the Low Place: a Poetic Journey

_____

_____

_____

_____

_____

_____

_____

_____

_____

_____

_____

_____

_____

Verified

1 Peter 2:9

It's true.
I always felt like I needed validation.
True.
I was unaware of my self-worth.
But that – I am no longer.
No longer do I have to search for
endorsement--- I'm backed by heaven.
I don't need admission to your cliques, the
God of Angel armies has a place for me.
Verification by the world's standards doesn't
compare to being written in the Book of Life.
I always felt like I needed validation. That was
not the truth.
I am accepted.
Acknowledged and approved.
Christ saw me at my lowest, even knowing
my flaws, looking beyond my faults, and saw my
needs. Still, He made room.
Not just room on the cross for me (He got up
there alone carrying my sins) and made room
in His heart. He got up there aware that I would
mess up.
I am loved.
Desired and adored.
Christ chose me, He preferred me amongst
others, selected – I was designated before the
beginning of time interwoven into history's plan
to be a part of Christ's royal lineage. Aforetime

God wanted a relationship with me, and HE made the first move.

I am cherished.

Those whom he predestined He also called. Those whom He called He also justified. Those whom He justified He also glorified.

His verification is my weapon against my own pride and insecurity. His verification enables, strengthens, and gives authority.

I am made well, full of wonder

There's no need to wander for any more answers

It is written, I am fearfully and wonderfully made.

This is my blue check, I am verified.

_____

_____

_____

_____

_____

_____

_____

_____

_____

_____

_____

_____

_____

Understand This

Psalm 139:14

Ayo, you mad pretty!
Yes, YOU are beautiful
What attracts me is the joy that leaps from
between your lips when you smile. The world
didn't give that to you and the world can't take
that away!
Yes, YOU with the gapped tooth,
I'm talking to you with the overbite, the
underbite, and the crooked smile. YOU with the
unibrow and your over-pronounced lips
DON'T YOU DARE hide behind that or those
scars.
I see you--
And you are mad pretty.
Girl! Don't you dare hide.
And don't you dare cry.
I'm going to need you to get reacquainted
with you.

Allow me to reintroduce you to me, you see, I
am YOU and you are ME.
I am beautiful
Say it with me out loud say, "I AM Beautiful"
I am sure that my worth is far beyond rubies.
I am secure in who He made me.
I don't need a mirror to tell me I am
beautiful. God's word already did.

_____

_____

_____

_____

_____

_____

_____

_____

_____

_____

_____

_____

_____

Fact vs Fiction

John 8:32

You will be able to tell in the structure of the words that I conjure up.

My voice will no longer carry its open pitch to ascend, comfort, and greet lies.

I KNOW THE TRUTH.

Everything will change.

You think that nothing has changed. Oh, but EVERYTHING has changed.

I KNOW THE TRUTH.

In this change, my heart will neither cry nor apologize for being overly sized, it's oversized

and this the enemy will not take.

I KNOW THE TRUTH.

I have feelings. I am human.

and those feelings are extremely valid. Yet still.

I KNOW THE TRUTH.

So, no matter what you say, no matter what they say

the decision has been made to cut ties; I KNOW THE TRUTH.

It's true that absence makes the heart grow fonder, but my heart does not need to be fond of fabrication

my heart does not need to be fond of deception

my heart does not need to be fond of falsification and lies. I KNOW THE TRUTH.

This is the end of a long-drawn-out era. There is only one King of my heart

There is only one true living God.

I once was lost but now I'm found. NOW I KNOW THE TRUTH.

Life in the Low Place: a Poetic Journey

_____

_____

_____

_____

_____

_____

_____

_____

_____

_____

_____

_____

_____

_____

Double U

Psalm 27 :13

It's Me vs. Me
Playing offense and defense. Passing the
time, I am waiting
Anticipating, abiding, marking the time,
watching, holding on, pausing, tarrying, standing
by, sitting tight, foreseeing, -- Waiting
Waiting happily. Waiting angrily. Waiting sad.
Waiting anxiously. Waiting patiently...Waiting
It's me vs. me
Playing offense and defense passing the time
I am wading.
Tearing into, working through, setting about,
tackling,
jumping in, going forward, initiating,
launching, plodding -- Wading
I waded ditches instead of finding easier
crossing places, I didn't want what was easy.
I was told that this was worth it.
So, I'm wading -- I toiled to get here
So, I'm wading -- I labored through emotions
So, I'm wading -- working for the future
Wading ...
It's me vs. me
Playing offense and defense, passing the
time
I am Winning.
I waited and waded for this W

because these W's are ones that'll humble
you
waiting with expectation
wading in the water
Update: **I won**

_____

_____

_____

_____

_____

_____

_____

_____

_____

_____

_____

_____

_____

Eventually, You Will Become

Hebrews 11:11

Eventually, you will become.
And I wonder what you will look like—in the future of course.
I pray that you have your father's eyes, spiritually and naturally He sees, he knows, he cares...
I pray that you have your mother's heart spiritually and naturally
A heart of flesh,
a heart that's open, a heart that feels.
I'm speaking to the future
Even in the terms as it was written You were made full of wonder
--wonderfully made.
You are a reminder that promises—
even when whispered in the rain will never wash away
So, as we wait for the arrival to see the promise and the potential fulfilled, I will believe the best for your life.
So please accept the best for your life.
Before you even had breath you were created in His image and offered eternity through sacrificial love
I have no doubt that by grace, through faith you will become.

Life in the Low Place: a Poetic Journey

Covenant

Deuteronomy 7 :9

Like a long-awaited victory, I anticipated Your coming
And when mustard seed faith just wasn't enough Still, I had hope for Your entrance
Joy bells oh joy bells they're ringing in my soul
Today is the day my arrow has landed
The Warrior, a Victor, The Seed a Son
The Mother, grateful
The hearts full
Wrapped in the blanket of God's love, I found warmth
Therein I found comfort
Reciting what my mind knew but my heart needed to hear
I said "God is not hard of hearing and is not reluctant to bless His children "
I learned a lesson in the valley even though I would gladly trade those lessons for the one that slipped away.
Though only a poppyseed in size the weight of grief was so ridiculously heavy.
Even still, healing had found a way to override the gloom of the storm many silently go through.
The promise maker is held above the promise and a covenant He will not break —
His goodness will carry you.
The load He will share with you.

He does not lie
There's a peace He provides
Rest here
 Cry here
Abide
For there is no shame in loss
Pick up your head
Joy is your portion
Healing is your portion
And the promise belongs to you
Is it not His promise that goodness and
mercy shall follow His children? Goodness—
His goodness.

Life in the Low Place: a Poetic Journey

_____

_____

_____

_____

_____

_____

_____

_____

_____

_____

_____

_____

Promising Colors

Genesis 9:13

If red never mattered before,
it matters even more now;
— the blood.

No need to arrange the range of burnt
orange and mellow yellow that blend as the sun
shines knowing that Christ lives, and Christ loves.

It's goodbye to burnt offerings because
the Son shined. He was the sacrifice and salvation
that met me with a hello.

And if that wasn't enough, He made me
lie down in green pastures and led me beside
quiet waters, ensuring peace that guaranteed my
security.

Gratitude for hues of blues that soothe
like ocean waves that obey its Creator. Because
fear of the Lord seeks to honor Him.

And oh, like Lydia, just as valuable purple
cloth, I was bought.

Ransomed in fact by love.

Listening closely, the Lord opened my heart
ensuring eternal life.

Life in the Low Place: a Poetic Journey

_____

_____

_____

_____

_____

_____

_____

_____

_____

_____

_____

_____

_____

Hope Postponed

Psalm 39:7

When you see me don't stare.
Don't look too hard—at these battle scars.
Just see me and know that I'm not there. I'm
not there anymore.
Do you know what a dream deferred looks
like?
Well, it starts with hope deferred
It looks like needles in balloons and a clock
crushing eggs
Do you know what a dream deferred sounds
like?
Well, it sounds like a puppy's whimper from a
stepped-on tail
like a high-pitched scream in slow motion
Here's the part where you realize that this is
not even a dream, in fact it's a nightmare.
The terror that night brings when hope is
lost, and faith is far is strictly the enemy's strategy
to trick you into believing that hope is lost.
I was a sleeping beauty,
and though I will dream again I am no longer
sleeping.
The child is not dead but asleep. Rise up.

Life in the Low Place: a Poetic Journey

_____

_____

_____

_____

_____

_____

_____

_____

_____

_____

_____

_____

_____

Real Love

Romans 8:35

Why do I love thee
One whom I've never met?

Why do you love me?
Even if in hell I made a bed.
Is it clay that you see?
Is it heaven that you hear?
Because only heaven would make me believe
That a cross is worthy to bear.
I did not deserve that—
But You laid down Your life for a friend.
You chose thorns instead for me.

Why do I love thee
One whom I've never met?

Though conversations sometimes one sided,
I can't say which of us did the most talking?
But if I'm honest, I wondered why You love me?
Though Your love is not a mystery,
I can't seem to see why You chose me.
Why You—
hold me.
Why You correct me,
how You know me,
But why do I blindly believe?

How did my 1, 2, 3 mustard seeds,
Grow into this steadfast tree that always abounds
in

Life in the Low Place: a Poetic Journey

Hope, love, and faith to thee —
I love You.

Though I've never seen Your face I know
it's beautiful.

And though I've never physically held your hand I
know it's strong.

You are God and You do no wrong.

Even though bad things sometimes happen to
good people,
I know I've seen it.

I lost way too many good things to count.
Yet still I know You don't count me out.

I know that's not what this love is about.
You gave me a million little miracles.
And tonight, I write in expectancy, in
hope.

In awe yet heart full, heart feeling,
waiting, wanting, wondering when it will be my
turn for another one.

Excuse my tone, Lord, but You know which one
I'm talking about.

_____

_____

_____

_____

_____

_____

_____

_____

_____

_____

_____

_____

_____

_____

The Voice of God

Ezekiel 43:2

I would be crazy to pretend that Zion wasn't
always calling me to a higher place of praise.
　　　For as long as I've been breathing there's
been a voice that has been constant even in its
silence.

　　　Some days I heard no voice, but the voice
was not absent.

　　　I heard it—I heard Him.
In the wind, a whistle almost pronounced my full
name once.

　　　Well, it did say, "Daughter" and it did say,
"Friend".

It sounded like it said, "Beautiful".
　　　All of those things pretty much describe
me, so it makes sense, He spoke to me.

　　　If I'm honest it's in the dark that I learned
whatever you give the most attention intensifies
the most in volume.
Had I never heard the voice of the Ancient of Days
I wouldn't know that the darkness tells lies.

LOUD LIES

Lies like, "You'll never live to see the promises".

Lies like, "You deserved every bad thing happened you".

Lies like, "You are not good enough".

Loud, Stupid, Nasty lies.

Lies that sound nothing like the wind because The Rock of Ages would never say those things, but this was so loud!

It spoke in my dreams - night terror.
It spoke to my shadows - condemnation of my past.

It even crept into my health - sickness and mental anguish.

The devil is a liar.

I shifted where my attention set then that's when I heard Him again. The Author, and the Finisher. The Perfecter. He speaks.

My ears were likely to hear where my energy was focused once again but this time it was a still, soft voice.

Who would've known that the voice of the wind could be so powerful?

Cushioned by His truth of course because His words do not return to Him void.

Life in the Low Place: a Poetic Journey

In the darkness the voice said: *Lo I will be with you always.* Matthew 28:20

In the darkness the voice said: *Seek the LORD and his strength; seek his presence continually!* 1 Chronicles 16:11

In the dark the voice said: *I will uphold you with my righteous right hand.* Isaiah 41:10

This was it! The tide had turned.
The City of David does not hide but lives within me!
Placed on the mountain of my heart where praise has to be offered in plenty and famine.

I heard Him speak to me—
I was low, and it was dark.
I heard Him speak to me—
Not only was He there too, but He cared enough to come get me.

The voice of God saved me.

It has raised my praise.

Life in the Low Place: a Poetic Journey

_____

_____

_____

_____

_____

_____

_____

_____

_____

_____

_____

_____

Sunday

Mark 16:9

I am sharing this to produce belief in the
truth, I am the proof that His blood works.
 You will know the truth of my past
 but there is one who knows the truth of my
future and on the third day early Sunday morning
 He got up for me
 You see,
 The very thing in my yesterday that kept me
away from Him was the very thing that made me a
recipient of His grace and a beneficiary of His
mercy
 Christ died for me.
 He sees,
 Every dent, every flaw, every mark, and even
the stains--
 I wiped my face and reproach, filled that rag,
I was dirty
 But he took those things, and *gospeled* them
like only a father could
He was patient on that cross, dying so that I could
live.
 And as for me,
 every puncture in his side, every tear in his
eye
 Every lash and every slash
Every nail and every whip was taken with me in
mind

Though rejected and abused, hurt, and accused
Guilty, confused, and all the more
The Gospel of Sunday is what reshaped my identity.
My soul was an orphan without the gospel.

Life in the Low Place: a Poetic Journey

_____

_____

_____

_____

_____

_____

_____

_____

_____

_____

_____

_____

_____

About the Poetess

Jazmyne Dodd, aka As Told by Mena, was born and raised in the city of Rochester, NY. Coming from a family of six, she is smack dab in the middle as her parents third child. Mena's love for writing is what she refers to as her "call to scribe". The passion for her writing is not found in the words alone but in the One who has anointed her to do so.

She subscribes to her faith and family as the most significant in her life. If she isn't spending time with family, you can almost always find Mena creating, and pouring into the next generation. She is a graphic designer with a leading-edge approach to various concepts and serves alongside her husband as Youth Pastor at Glory House International in Rochester, NY.

Life in the Low Place is the first of many stories from As Told by Mena.

www.ingramcontent.com/pod-product-compliance
Lightning Source LLC
Chambersburg PA
CBHW071105090426
42737CB00013B/2491

9780578930763